The Pillow Men

A Play By

D. L. Arber

About the Author

D. L. Arber, writer, actor and poet, was born in Illinois and grew up in Colorado, United States of America. He is a 2005 graduate of the University of Northern Colorado in Theatre Arts. As a student he performed in numerous school productions and also participated in New York University's summer theatre program. Following graduation he worked on stage, both as an actor and a producer, and in television in New York and Los Angeles, before returning to Colorado. In recent years he has been involved in writing both short stories and poetry.

"The Pillow Men" is a Play written by author, poet and actor D. L. Arber. Previously on television and the stage, D. L. Arber has focused his creativity on one of his strongest passions, playwriting.

Currently living in Colorado after time spent growing up in Illinois, NYC and Los Angeles, D. L. Arber's "The Pillow Men" shares with the reader an example of his work generated in 2017.

Character List

Wayne – A man in his 40's. Dark black hair. Wears a trench coat.

Jake – A man in his 30's. Blonde hair. Wears a military jacket.

Woman 1 – Voice of intercom, At Airport Podium, a Servant.

Woman 2 - A servant, gate attendant.

Flight Attendant - A young woman in her 20's.

Pilot Voice – Voiceover.

Hotel Attendant - A man in his late 20's in uniform.

Warehouse Man – A man with a clipboard and pen in his 20's.

An American Driver – A Taxi Driver.

A German Driver – A Taxi Driver.

Man on Intercom – An announcement made in an airport.

Policeman 1 – A White House Police Officer.

Policeman 2 – A White House Police Officer.

Synopsis of Scenes

Act IV

Act I, Scene I Brandenburg Airport Berlin Germany.

We open on an airport with busy passengers all in lines waiting to board the planes on the runway. Wayne, a tall man in his 40's has dark black hair and a long tan trench coat stands in the middle of the airport awaiting the arrival of a plane so he can board. All around him are passengers and people. He looks at his watch.

Wayne. (Out loud) 3:30pm.

Wayne checks the boards for his flight and looks at his ticket. Looking up, he hears a woman on the intercom announce his flight and state to begin boarding in twenty minutes.

Intercom: Flight 227 will begin boarding in twenty minutes.

Wayne stands while the people begin to get the bags together and get in line to board the plane. Just then another man, Jake enters and approaches Wayne. Jake, a man in his late 30's holds a piece of luggage and is tall with a large coat on. His hair is a mess, uncombed, blown by the wind outside.

Wayne. What took you so long?

Jake. I'll tell you later.

Wayne. Tell me now.

Jake. It was a woman. Outside, she asked for my number. I didn't give her anything, so she got angry and threw her hairbrush at me.

Wayne. The wind, you have a comb?

Jake. Yeah.

Wayne. Well we are boarding shortly.

Jake. (Looking at his watch) At 4pm?

Wayne. It was before that. Let's get in the line.

Both move as if standing in a line and stand one behind another. Each of them holds a carry on bag.

Jake. We are almost home.

Wayne. Keep tight. We are going to make it.

Jake. Keep your fingers crossed tight.

Wayne. They're so tight, I can't feel 'em.

Just then a woman voice on the intercom starts to speak and begins to board the flight.

Woman on Intercom. Flight 227 to Washington D. C. will now begin boarding. Please have your tickets ready.

Both begin to slowly make their way to the front of the line to the entrance to the runway.   As a stage effect, the stage manager should have a group of people form a line from stage left running to stage right.   While the line moves, the two characters Wayne and Jake will move with them, until finally boarding stage left. Moving from right to left, they will speak their dialogue. After about a minute they make their way to stage right and approach the flight attendant.

Woman at Gate. Tickets please.

Wayne hands her his ticket. The woman looks at him a moment as he hands him his ticket. She pauses for a moment and then hands him his ticket.

Woman. Danka shein.

Wayne. Danka.

Jake approaches and hands the woman his ticket. She looks at him.

Woman. Are you two...together?

Jake. We are close friends.

Woman. I see. Enjoy your flight.

Jake. Danka.

The two men exit stage left with their bags.

End Scene.

Act I, Scene II Plane Cabin.

We open on the interior of an airplane as there are passengers finishing boarding the plane and finding their seats. The passenger plane is a laid out as a passenger plane on stage as there are two separate rows of passengers with an aisle in the middle, forming two rows of passengers where Wayne and Jake are seated in the first row on the "Window Seat and the aisle. There are two seats are placed per side and is laid out with an aisle and a total of four seats to make up the interior cabin seating arrangement.

Wayne. It is cold.

Jake. Ask for a blanket and a pillow.

Wayne. Well done.

Jake. Do you think the pillows on the plane are worth anything?

Wayne. Only if we were flying with the president or a VIP plane would something be worth anything.

Jake. What if I had my own private jet? Would the pillows be worth anything then?

Wayne. We are talking about your own plane? Yours?

Jake. Yes.

Wayne. No.

Jake. You are very funny. I consider myself a very important person.

Wayne. As do I. Dead or alive.

Just then the pilot comes on an intercom announces the flight and the time and destination and speaks.

Pilot. Flight 227 to Washington D. C. Our trip will be a 4170 mile flight that should put us in Washington D. C. by 6am. Flight attendants will be around in a minute to check your belts and make sure we are flight ready. We will be cruising at an altitude between 32 and 33 thousand feet at an air temperature of -45 degrees Fahrenheit, so no jumping! Fasten your seatbelts. As a reminder this is a non-smoking flight.

A flight attendant comes out of the wing and down the aisle.

Attendant. Fasten your seatbelts.

Everyone settles and is ready for takeoff. Wayne and Jake sit next to one

another downstage right. These are spacious
seats. Both have ample room.

Wayne. We will be home in no time.

Jake. Yee haw.

End Scene.

Act I, Scene III Earlier Flashback Scene Moscow.

Flashback. Earlier. On the run, we see the two thieves, Wayne and Jake carrying briefcases and large pieces of luggage that are large. We see them carrying them through a darkened stage, from stage left to right, running, hurrying over hills and through buildings. Jake follows Wayne in and around the stage. Upstage to downstage and they travel through the cities making a stop in each to steal. Here they arrive in Moscow as they both have a plan to make a stop at the Kremlin.

Wayne. Hurry!

Jake. I'm here!

Wayne. Well, stay close. I have the exact coordinates. We are close!

Jake. Can't we work on something like jewelry? Or silver, gold? I mean of all things to heist, why can't it be money or something?

Wayne. Because this is more important. Besides, no would ever think of a thing like this. And we will stay ahead of the authorities. And no one would ever suspect. When we get back to the U. S. we will have one heck of a story to tell!

Jake. I'm with you all the way!

The two run downstage to the left and then across to stage right. They turn around and look out into the audience. They make there way back to backstage where they hurry across as the lights flash of lightening and thunder and the sound of rain. They make their way across the stage and we see screens along the backdrop where there are pictures shown for each city that is visited. Shown is a picture of St. Basil's Cathedral. then the Kremlin. The two hurry downstage right.

Wayne. Okay. We are here. Here is the plan. We pose as armed guards. Then we make an entrance. We will watch for the security officers and then make an entrance to the building during dinner. Then we will be able to get out without notice.

Jake. I follow.

Wayne. Yes.

Lights come up on the two men as they make their way off stage left as the set changes to an interior room of the Kremlin. They make way through to a bedroom where there is a bed. There is a bed on stage with pillows on top. The two slowly make their way to the front of the bed where they each take a pillow and press it firmly to their body, do to their large coats they can fit them underneath and walk out. Both exit stage left with a pillow in hand.

The lights dim and the two come downstage both with a pillow under their coats. They talk to one another.

Wayne. Got em!

Jake. Yeah!

Wayne. Well done. Well done. We must go. We cannot stay here.

Jake. Let's go.

As the lights dim, the two make their way to the rear of the stage and then off stage. They take the pillows with them. Lights fade to black.
End Scene.

Act I, Scene IV Sheremetyevo International
Airport.

There is a line from stage right to stage
left. Wayne and Jake stand in line with two
pieces of luggage with them. The line moves
from left to right off stage as the two begin to
board another plane. The two approach
stage left entrance and they give tickets to a
woman at the exit. The woman who stands at
the exit speaks over an intercom.

Woman. Boarding flight 353 to
London. Please have your tickets ready.

The two men get out their tickets. They
both look like they are in need of a rest. It is
late at night and it seems like there is no order
to things. The woman speaks again.

Woman. We will be boarding at 2am sharp. Estimated flight arrival time to London: 3 hours. Traveling Distance 1,555 miles.

The two men exit stage left as if to board the plane. They come down stage to an arranged plane set as before where there is an aisle and two rows of seating for Wayne and Jack and they find their seats with tickets in hand where there are people seated and one more to follow.

Wayne. It's not long. We have only a few hours until arrival. We can rest in the meantime. We have checked our bags. They should be fine. Everything is hidden away.

Jake. Where to afterward? We still have 3 more stops to make don't we? I think there would be a chance we could do the jobs pretty fast right? I mean one pillow at a time. We will find a way.

Wayne. Yes. We have to make London first.   Then afterward we will decide what is best, which destination we will go to first. After, we make all three stops we will return home.

Jake. Well, I think we should go to Germany last. If I have a say in anything, I say hold off on Germany until the very end.

Wayne. I will take that into consideration.

The woman comes on the intercom again.

Woman. Please fasten your seatbelts and store all bags underneath the seats for safety.

The pilot comes on the intercom and speaks in Russian.

Wayne. Did you get that?

Jake. Every word.

Wayne. (Laughing) Ha ha ha!!!

Jake.   The leaders won't know what hit them!

Wayne. You got that right.

Jake. Well, we are off to London.

Wayne. See the sites.

Jake. (Whispering) TAKE the pillows!

End Scene

Act I, Scene V London International Airport.

We hear the whoosh of an airplane on the tarmac as several pass in the air. There is a sound of planes arriving and departing in the airport as Wayne and Jake appear in London's Heathrow airport. Wayne and Jake carry two bags with them and go to claim their baggage, the pieces that carry the pillows inside. The enter stage left carrying two bags each, one with personal belongings and the other a presidential pillow. The two come downstage center.

Wayne. We are here. We have not very far to go. We must find a place to ship the contents of our bags home. We cannot travel with several pillows. We shouldn't even have them on us!

Jake. Check.

Wayne. After we obtain the queens pillow, we will go to a parcel service and ship every pillow we have thus far, home.

Jake. Right-O.

Wayne. Is there an easier way?

Jake. I see your point. Ok. I follow.

Wayne. As the sun sets, we will enter the grounds at 10 downing street and obtain the pillows. Two in all.

Jake. The Prime Minister!!??

Wayne. Yes.

Jake. Well, I suppose he will survive. They ARE only pillows.

Wayne. But they are very important pillows! Presidential pillows!

Jake. Ok. Well I really don't want to get caught! I mean, what happens? How do we get in there?

Wayne. Follow the signs my friend. The signs will lead us right to her.

Jake. Okay. Let's go.

Wayne.   Taxi!

End Scene

Act I, Scene VI Hotel in London.

The two exit stage and we hear the honk of a taxi driver and they whoosh off into the wee hours of the morning. Before noon, they arrive close to 10 Downing Street and check into a nearby hotel. They bring their luggage inside. Upon arriving there is a hotel attendant waiting to check them in. The two enter stage and approach a counter where the attendant stands.

Wayne. We would like a room for two please.

Jake. For two.

Attendant. Very well. We can arrange that. One bed or two?

Wayne. Two! Do you think we would sleep in the same bed?

Attendant. Just a question sir. No problem. That can be arranged.

Wayne. Cheers.

Attendant. Ok. We have one here. I have a two bed available on the 22nd floor. How does that sound?

Wayne. Wonderful. Is there breakfast in the morning?

Attendant. Why yes. There will be breakfast served in the mornings at 7am.

Wayne. Great. We will take it. Thanks.

Jake. We will.

Wayne. Quiet! I'll handle it.

Attendant. May I see an ID?

Wayne shows the ID and then the attendant hands Wayne the keys to the room and Wayne signs a piece of paper. Wayne and Jake exit stage.

End Scene.

Act II, Scene I Hotel Room Night.

Wayne and Jake make their way into a hotel room and there are two beds where they both sit down their luggage. There is a lamp and a table with a bible inside the drawer. The window looks out over London Bridge. There are curtains backstage that show the skyline of London through the curtains. It is quiet and the two speak.

Wayne. Ok. We have a few minutes. Let's put the bags away and get ready to travel to Downing Street. It is close-by. We can walk. We will sleep here tonight and then in the morning we will obtain the pillows. We will check out tomorrow morning and get breakfast and then off to pinch the pillows.

Jake. Did you say breakfast?

Wayne. Didn't you hear the attendant?

Jake. Yummy. I can't wait!

Wayne. Well, we can make it there before the day gets on. Let's make it fast, quick and clean! I don't need the patrol coming after me.

Jake. And then off to the airport?

Wayne. Yes. Then we are off to Greece. It is a night flight. Tomorrow night. We have to make this pinch and be gone before anyone knows about it.

Jake. Check. I am with you all the way.

Wayne. Dawn.

The lights go out.

End Scene.

Act II, Scene II Hotel, London.

Morning. Wayne and Jake enter the stage and go to an attendant that stands at a counter. The attendant smiles and speaks with Wayne. Jake follows along.

Attendant. That will be $249.50 please.

Wayne. One night?

Attendant. Yes.

Wayne. Here you go. (He hands the attendant a card and then signs a piece of paper.) And where is the breakfast?

Attendant. Just off that way. Have a pleasant day.

Wayne. We plan to. Thank you.

Jake. Pancakes!

Wayne. Black Pudding Jake. Haven't you heard?

Jake. I'll have to try it.

Wayne. But of course!

The two exit.

Act II, Scene III London Street.

Wayne and Jake make their way to Downing Street.   We hear crowds and noises from the stage as they travel in the early morning sun to make it toward the palace. We see lights and sights from a screen on the back wall. There are pictures of London being shown and the image of the sun in the sky. Wayne and Jake walk down stage and across the stage, the back to the left to make as though they are walking the distance from the hotel to the palace. There is a sign in place that has signs in shapes of arrows that point in every direction. One says 10 Downing Street.

Wayne. This way.

Jake. Right-O.

Wayne. Let's go.

Jake. You lead.

Wayne. We will stop on the side and make our way in. It is the only way.

Jake. Okay.

Wayne. We will get everything. 1 pillow each. Follow me.

The two make their way around the stage in a circle. They then exit. They then re-enter and there is a guard that stands downstage left. With bags in hand, they cross behind the guard slowly as not to be seen.

Wayne. Sssshhh! Quiet!

They quickly make their way off stage not being seen by the guard.

End Scene

Act II, Scene IV Inside 10 Downing Street London.

The two enter the stage where a bed lies with two pillows on them. They enter stage left and look at the bed. Just then they hear two women speaking from off stage right. There is laughter and then hearing them, the two quickly hide underneath the beds. The two women enter.

Woman 1. Fine morning.

Woman 2. Sunshine.

Woman 1. I think we should have a nice day as the prince and queen are out.

Woman 2. Yes, there should be a nice lunch planned shortly.

Woman 1. Lovely. Perhaps we can sit out on the terrace.

Woman 2. It probably can be arranged.

Woman 1. Mr. Cameron looked wonderful this morning didn't he?

Woman 2. Yes. Dressed very nice.

Woman 1. Here, straighten the sheets, and let's make our way down stairs to prepare for lunch.

Woman 2. Very well.

The woman walk around the bed, straightening the sheet. They walk to the left, tucking in the sheets under the pillows and then they tuck the sheets under the mattress at the end of the bed and then brush off the top. There is a covering that reaches all the way around the base of the bed so to cover the space between the ground and the bed, covering it up. The two men underneath the bed are not seen because of it. The two women, once finished, exit the stage. Once they are gone, and it is a minute or so, the two men slowly make their way out from under the bed and stand. They whisper to one another.

Jake. That was close!

Wayne. That's for sure.

Jake. They were making me hungry too!

Wayne. Well, I am sorry to say we won't be going to lunch with them.

Jake. Shucks!

Wayne. Quick, no is our chance! Get the pillows!

Jake. Right!

The two go to the bed and remove the two pillows from the top. One is the Prime Minister Mr. David Cameron's, the other is of his wife Samantha Cameron. Wayne and Jake take the pillows, fold them and fit them into the bags they are carrying. Once done, they look around, and then Jake follows Wayne off stage quietly.

Wayne. C'mon! Let's go quickly!

Jake. I am right behind you!

End Scene

Act II Scene V Shipping Warehouse London.

Sounds of airplanes as the lights are dark. On the screen in the back are projected images of planes and locations like that of London, Moscow, Germany or Greece. There are sounds of people and newspaper headlines thrown like an EXTRA EXTRA along the screen. There are sounds of police and sirens in the background. The lights come up on a shipping warehouse. The two thieves enter the stage approach a man working. He is writing something on a clipboard. Wayne and Jake approach.

Man. May I help you?

Wayne. Yes, we would like to ship two of our bags please.

Man. Ok. What is the destination?

Wayne. The United States of America.

Man.   Very well. May I see some ID?

Wayne. (Showing some ID to the man.) Sure.

Man. You look familiar. Do we know each
other?

Wayne. Don't think so.

Man. Well, I am sure I have seen your face
somewhere.

Wayne. Not sure.

Man. Hmm. Not sure. Well, you sure look
familiar! Maybe I will think of it.

Wayne. Maybe.

Man. Well, we can ship both bags to the U. S. for a fee of $180.00 American dollars.

Wayne. Sounds good.

Man. What's inside?

Wayne. Just some personal items, some clothing.

Man. Very well. When do you need it there by?

Wayne. Saturday.

Man. And the city?

Wayne. Washington D. C.

Man. Will you be traveling there?

Wayne. No. We have some other sites to see first.

Jake. Two more!

Man. I see. Sign here.

Wayne signs. The two leave the two large bags with them. The pillows are inside. Wayne and Jake then leave the stage.   The man puts a tag on the bags and writes on his clipboard.

End Scene.

Act III, Scene I London International Airport.

Sounds of planes and whooshing from an airport. The two enter the stage with now only 1 bag each to take with them on the plane. There is a woman downstage left as they enter. The two men approach.

Woman. Athens. 6pm flight.

Wayne. That's us!

Jake. Yes!

Woman. Ticket's please!

Handing here two tickets the woman inspects. She hands them back.

Woman. The flight is now boarding.

Wayne. Jake, let's go!

Jake. Right here boss!

The two exit stage. The lights fade. The sounds of planes and takeoff noises continue. A large Whoosh is heard as a plane takes off.

End Scene.

Act III, Scene II Athens International Airport, Greece.

Sounds of planes and travel. The two men enter the stage. They each carry a bag. They walk center stage.

Wayne. Athens. I have always wanted to travel here. I just never thought it would be for pillows. But it has to be done. Let's not take long. Let's be persistent.

Jake. It is warm. What will we carry them in, we don't have our bags? I have a tie; we can fold them and carry them. No one will notice they are presidential. It will be like we have gone camping.

Wayne. Good idea! Great Jake!

Jake. We have the whole day. Let's not waste any time.

Wayne. Central Athens, here we come.

Jake. Taxi!

Wayne. Good work. Taxi!

The sound of a horn honking is heard. The two exit the stage.

End Scene

Act III, Scene III Athens, Greece Presidential Mansion.

We see a mansion on the screen on the back wall. It is the Presidential Mansion, where the president lives. Wayne and Jake enter the stage.

Wayne. The presidential mansion!

Jake. Wow. We actually made it this far. This is going to take longer than a day.

Wayne. No one will suspect us. We can do it.

Jake. It is a beautiful palace.

Wayne. Reminds me of the White House.

Jake. Won't we be going there too?

Wayne. One place at time. Yes. We have two other stops. Berlin's Bellevue Palace and the White House. If you know, there is a new president of Greece since 2015. His name is Prokopis Pavlopoulos. He has only been in office for a little over a year. He is the seventh president of Greece.

Jake. I see. And we are taking his pillows.

Wayne. Yes Jake. Both his and his wife's.

Jake. Well, we are close. How do we get in?

Wayne. I have researched this place several times. There is a side entrance that leads directly to the bedrooms. We will get the pillows there. It shouldn't be too difficult. I will need your ties. We will have to pretend as though they are our pillows. We will slip out unnoticed! Clean and quick!

Jake. You lead, I will follow.

Wayne. Okay. Let's go.

The two exit stage and proceed to enter the building. Lights go out.

End Scene.

Act III Scene IV A Bedroom in the Palace.

Wayne and Jake enter stage to a bedroom where there is a large bed made. There is no one around. They quickly go to the bed, remove the pillows and fold them and tie them up in a folding fashion.

Wayne. Here. The ties.

Jake. Right. Slide them over.

The two fold the pillows and put them under their arms. They look at the bed and scan the area. There is no one. They quickly move to exit.

Wayne. Right.

Jake. Get moving!

Wayne. Don't tell me what to do. Quick.
Good. Now, let's go. To the Taxi!

The two exit the stage and the lights go out.

End Scene.

Act III, Scene V Athens International Airport.

Lights come up. The two make their way on stage in an airport. There is the sound of planes and sounds of people. Wayne and Jake stand in line. A woman comes on the intercom.

Woman. Athens to Berlin. 5 Hour Flight time. Distance: 1455 Miles. All boarding, please have your tickets ready.

Wayne. Ok. Last stop and then we are on our way home to the good ole U. S of A.

Jake. Can't we steal a BMW or something? Why in the heck does it have to be pillows?

Wayne. A pillow gives a person comfort. A pillow is a sign of wealth! Many people in civilizations before us went without pillows. In our modern life, we have pillows to keep comfortable and remind us of our wealth!

Jake. You are right. I don't like sleeping without a pillow. I can't imagine what they used to do without them. I can see why they were invented!

Wayne. Well now. I think there a pillow could also be a way to a woman's soul!

Jake. Really?

Wayne. You'll have to ask a woman Jake. Don't you know any women?

Jake. Not really.

Wayne. Well, it's time to change that.

Jake. Maybe when we get back to the United States.

Wayne.   Definitely!

Woman. We like pillows. I will say that.

Tickets please!

Wayne and Jake reach the woman at the entrance to the plane. They hand over the tickets.

Woman. Danka.

Wayne. Danka.

Jake. Danka!

The two men exit the stage and make their way to the plane off stage left.

Woman. Enjoy your trip!

End Scene

Act III, Scene VI Brandenburg Airport, Germany.

The sounds of planes fill the stage. There is a screen projection of a Germany and different pictures of the places they have visited. There is perhaps even a picture of pillows that the two have been stealing from each leader of the countries they have visited. The two men enter to center stage.

Wayne. Ahh... Berlin. Our final stop before the White House.

Jake. The White House?

Wayne. Yes. Don't you know? This stop is our last international city. We are in foreign territory. After we must head to our domestic land.

Jake. How many more pillows do we need?

Wayne. Ah yes! I am glad you asked. So far
we have 6, two from each country. And we
are destined for a total of 10 pillows altogether.
Two more, herein Berlin and then the final two
will come from the White House.

Jake. Domestic Soil.

Wayne. Our land! Our grounds! Our country.

Jake. The United States of America!

Wayne. Yes!

Jake. So, where are we going here in
Germany? Berlin is a big place.

Wayne. How do you know?

Jake. Well, just a hunch.
Wayne. You are correct.

Jake. Where are we going?

Wayne. To the Bellevue Palace. Schloss Bellevue. It is where the president resides. Mr. Joachim Gauck himself.

Jake. Very well.

Wayne. So we must travel from the airport to the Palace. Distance is approximately 19 miles. And we are to travel by taxi.

Jake. Well, I am not walking.

Wayne. (Turning to the Audience) Taxi!

End Scene

Act III, Scene VII German Taxi.

A man with a chair arrives to resemble a taxi. He uses the chair and two others to "make" a Taxi that holds two passengers and a driver. The 3 chairs face the audience as the man as a driver faces the audience and speaks.

Driver. Halo!

Wayne. Yes. Hello.

Driver. Get in. And where are we off to?

Wayne. Take us to the Bellevue Palace. Schloss Bellevue.

Driver. Very Well. Presidential I must say.

Wayne. We must go there quick. How long will it take.

Driver. Oh, I would say approximately 30 minutes.

Wayne. Good. Take us there. We are on official business.

Jake. Official!

Driver. Very well.

Wayne. Thank you. This is my businessman, Jake.

Driver. Halo, Jake.

Jake. Um. Uh. Hello. Yes. Ahem. Hello!

Wayne. Is it possible you can wait for us when we arrive? We just have to pick something up there and then we will return. Can you wait for us outside?

Driver. It will have to be down the street. I can stop at the park. They won't allow people to park just outside.

Wayne. Good. The park. Take us there.

Driver. Very well.

The driver simulates driving. They drive a while and the screen on the back wall changes to different pictures and destinations and places the two have already been from famous places to simple pictures of beauty. After about a minute, he speaks.

Driver. Ok. The Bellevue Palace on the right. We stop at Teirgarten Park.

Wayne. Very good driver. I like your style. Quick and responsive.

Jake. (Getting out of the taxi stage left.)
Wow. Look at this place. Amazing!

Wayne. Keep your bag and get your ties.
Thanks driver. We shouldn't be long; we must
stop in the front and go right in. Then we
shouldn't be longer than 1 hour. How long can
you stay?

Driver. I will wait. But I will run the meter!

Wayne. Fine. We will be quick. Jake, let's go!

The two exit stage as the driver sits in the front
chair downstage right reading a newspaper.
He sits there through the scene and waits for
them to return. As the two exit the stage, we
hear German Palace music playing as they are
fast and we hear Wayne speak to Jake from
off stage in the wings.

Wayne. Hurry! C'mon! Let's go!

Jake. On my way!

Wayne. Now the pillows! The Pillows!

Just then Wayne and Jake re-enter the stage and in a zig zag direction make their way across stage, downstage and then to the Taxi driver who sits reading his paper downstage right.

Wayne. (to the driver) Ok! We have what we need. We are ready to return to the airport. Can you take us there?

Driver. Yes. No sights?

Wayne. I am afraid it will have to wait until next time.

Driver. Very well. Get in.

Wayne and Jake "Enter" the cab and the two simulate driving as they "travel" to return to Brandenburg Airport. All three sit as the driver drives. After a little while, Jake speaks.

Jake. Are we there yet?

Driver. 5 minutes.

Wayne. Good. Drop us off in front.

After a couple of more minutes driving, the driver simulates "pulling over."

Driver. That will be 35 Euros gents!

Wayne. Good. Here you are. My card.

Driver. Thank you my good man. Enjoy your trip.

Wayne. Thank you friend.

Wayne and Jake exit the Taxi and walk to up stage left. They make a turn and another turn to simulate a longer distance to walk. From Downstage right to upstage Left. Both exit the stage.

End Scene.

Act IV, Scene I Flashback Act I, Scene I
Brandenburg Airport, Germany.

We open on an airport with busy
passengers all in lines waiting to board the
planes on the runway. Wayne stands. All
around him are passengers and people. He
looks at his watch.

Wayne. (Out loud) 3:30pm.

Wayne checks the boards for his flight
and looks at his ticket.   Looking up, he hears a
woman on the intercom announce his flight
and state to begin boarding in twenty minutes.

Intercom: Flight 227 will begin
boarding in twenty minutes.

Wayne stands while the people begin to
get the bags together and get in line to board
the plane.   Just then another man, Jake enters

and approaches Wayne. Jake, a man in his late 30's holds a piece of luggage and is tall with a large coat on. His hair is a mess, uncombed, blown by the wind outside.

Wayne. What took you so long?

Jake. I'll tell you later.

Wayne. Tell me now.

Jake. It was a woman. Outside, she asked for my number. I didn't give her anything, so she got angry and threw her hairbrush at me.

Wayne. The wind, you have a comb?

Jake. Yeah.

Wayne. Well we are boarding shortly.

Jake. (Looking at his watch) At 4pm?

Wayne. Before that. Let's get in the line.

Both move as if standing in a line and stand one behind another. Each of them holds a carry on bag.

Jake. We are almost home.

Wayne. Keep tight. We are going to make it.

Jake. Keep your fingers crossed tight.

Wayne. They're so tight, I can't feel 'em.

Just then a woman voice on the intercom starts to speak and begins to board the flight.

Woman on Intercom. Flight 227 to Washington D. C. will now begin boarding. Please have your tickets ready.

Both begin to slowly make their way to the front of the line to the entrance to the runway. As a stage effect, the stage manager should have a group of people form a line from stage left running to stage right. While the line moves, the two characters Wayne and Jake will move with them, until finally boarding stage left. Moving from right to left, they will speak their dialogue. After about a minute they make their way to stage right and approach the flight attendant.

Woman at gate. Tickets please.

Wayne hands her his ticket. The woman looks at him a moment as he hands him his ticket. She pauses for a moment and then hands him his ticket.

Woman. Danka shein.

Wayne. Danka.

Jake approaches and hands the woman his ticket. She looks at him.

Woman. Are you two...together?

Jake. We are close friends.

Woman. I see. Enjoy your flight.

Jake. Danka.

The two men exit stage left with their bags.

End Scene.

Act IV, Scene II Reagan National Airport.

Sounds of airplanes and travel. The screen projects images. The two men enter the stage each with a bag in hand. On the intercom a man speaks.

Man on Intercom. Welcome to Reagan National Airport! The time is now 6am. Have a wonderful day!

Wayne and Jake make their way downstage. They stop to speak.

Wayne. Ah yes! The wonderful United States of America! I am so happy to be back on domestic soil! We have made it this far and we only have a little bit further to go. Are you prepared my friend?

Jake. Yes. I am ready. One more set of pillows. This time from the President of the United States!

Wayne. Yes Jake. Then we are to head home. We will keep the pillows as tokens of our work and labor abroad.

Jake. We are off to The White House?

Wayne. Yes Jake. You are correct. You know exactly where we are going. What's the address?

Jake. 1600 Pennsylvania Avenue.

Wayne. Yes. Right! Let's get catch a cab. Taxi!

A man with 3 chairs enters from stage right. He carries the chairs to downstage right. He

sets them up and motions for the men to get
in.

Driver. Get in!

Wayne and Jake sit down on their chairs. It is a
makeshift taxi, as it was in previous scenes.
The three sit. The driver drives.

Driver. Hey guys. Where to?

Wayne. The White House.

Driver. Sure! Shouldn't be long!

Wayne. How long will it take?

Driver. About 15 minutes. It's nice this
morning. We shouldn't have much trouble.

Wayne. Great!

Jake. 1600 Pennsylvania Avenue.

Wayne. We have a new president.

Jake. We sure do. And a new first lady!

Driver. I have calculated, and it is only 4 miles
from the airport to the president's house.

Wayne. Sounds good. Can you drop us off
right in front?

Driver. I don't think that can be done. It is not
allowed.

Wayne. Well, can you please take us to the
closest drop off location?

Driver. That, I can do.

Jake. Can we get breakfast first?

Wayne. That may be a good idea. What would America be without breakfast? Driver, can you take us to a local place where they serve breakfast?

Driver. I know a great place and it is on the way. In fact it is walking distance from the White House. After breakfast you can simply walk on over there. It is called Wicked Waffle. It is about a five minute walk to The White House.

Wayne. Sounds good. I would love to go there.

Jake. Me too! Wicked Waffles. I love waffles. Given, I like French toast better. But Waffles will do.

Wayne. Sounds good. Driver! Take us there.

Driver. Will do! Sit back and relax!

Wayne and Jake wait. In a moment the driver stops.

Driver. Here we are! That will be 25.50.

Wayne. For 15 minutes?

Driver. Yes sir.

Wayne. Alright. Here you are.

Wayne and Jake exit the taxi. They walk off stage left.

End Scene.

Act IV, Scene III The White House, U. S. A.

Wayne and Jake make their way to the front of the stage. They both look up and at one another. They have had breakfast and have walked from Wicked Waffles to 1600 Pennsylvania Avenue. They stop to talk.

Wayne. Well, here we are.

Jake. Yea!

Wayne. We have to be careful. This is a highly guarded location and probably the most difficult to get in to.

Jake. How do we do it?

Wayne. Follow me.

Wayne begins to walk upstage when just then two patrol men stop them in their tracks. They have guns in their hands and speak to Wayne and Jake.

Police 1. Get down! On the ground!

Police 2. I know you guys. The Pillow Men! We have seen you two on the news. You travel all across the world stealing pillows from presidential figures? And now the White House! Well, no more! We have you just where we want you!

Wayne. Wait! You have the wrong guy! You have the wrong men!

Police 1. Yea? We seized your package coming in from London. We know who you are. You two are finished!

Police 2. Say goodbye to the Pillow men!

Jake. No! No!

Wayne. No!

The two patrolmen bring the men around front and put them in handcuffs. Wayne and Jake respond with more "No's" as the patrol hold them in custody.

Police 1. You two pillow thieves are under arrest!

Police 2. You two are going to jail.

The End.

Acknowledgements

I would like to thank those that inspired me to begin writing again and helped me remember that there is always room for suspense. I would like to thank my parents for giving me the gift of life and an education and above all I would like to thank God for his grace and help along the way.

Props List:

2 White Standard Sized Pillows

2 Small Carry-on Bags

2 Suitcases

1 Steering Wheel (Detached)

2 Large Sized Airline Tickets

1 Pair of Handcuffs

Fake Money/ Euros and Dollars

Set List:

4 Chairs (Various Uses)

2 Twin Sized Beds (Can be put together to form one)

1 Wooden Podium

1 Screen with Projector for Pictures and Images

Made in United States
North Haven, CT
30 January 2024

48115545R00050